WHS

NATIONAL TESTS practice papers

FOR THE YEAR 2005

Maths Optional Tests
Levels 2–4

practice papers

AGE
8–9
Year 4

First published in 2005
exclusively for WHSmith by
Hodder Murray,
a member of the Hodder Headline Group
338 Euston Road
London NW1 3BH

Authors: Steve Mills and Hilary Koll

Impression   5   4   3   2   1
Year   2006   2005

Printed and bound in Spain

A catalogue record for this title is available from the British Library

ISBN 0 340 88865 2

NOTE: The tests, questions and advice in this book are not reproductions of the official test materials sent to schools. The official testing process is supported by guidance and training for teachers in setting and marking tests and interpreting the results. The results achieved in the tests in this book may not be the same as are achieved in the official tests.

Contents

The National Tests: A Summary

What are the National Tests?

Children who attend state schools in England sit National Tests (SATs) at the ages of 7, 11 and 14. Those at ages 11 and 14 are taken at the beginning of May. Those at age 7 can be carried out at any point during the year as chosen by the teacher. Children in Wales may take the same tests at 11 and 14 respectively. All children may also sit optional tests in the intervening years – many schools have chosen to adopt these tests.

The results are used by the school to assess each child's level of knowledge and progress in English and Maths at Key Stage 1 and English, Maths and Science at Key Stages 2 and 3. They also provide useful guidance for the child's next teacher.

The educational calendar for children aged 5–14 is structured as follows:

Key Stage	Year	Age by end of year	National Test
1 (KS1)	1	6	
	2	7	KEY STAGE 1
2 (KS2)	3	8	Optional Year 3
	4	9	Optional Year 4
	5	10	Optional Year 5
	6	11	KEY STAGE 2
3 (KS3)	7	12	
	8	13	
	9	14	KEY STAGE 3

Test Timetable

The Key Stage 1 National Tests have so far been carried out in May but, from the school year beginning September 2004, teachers will be allowed greater flexibility as to when they test the children and which tests or tasks they use. Key Stage 1 tests are now based on teacher assessment and can take place at any point during the year as chosen by the teacher.

Key Stage 2 tests take place in one week in May. All children sit the same test at the same time. In 2005, the tests will take place in the week of **9–13 May**. Your child's school will be able to provide you with a detailed timetable.

Key Stage 3 students will sit their tests on **3–6 May**.

Levels

National average levels have been set for children's results in the National Tests. The levels are as follows:

LEVEL	AGE 7 (KS1)	AGE 11 (KS2)	AGE 14 (KS3)
8			
7			
6			
5			
4			
3			
2			
2a			
2b			
2c			
1			

☐ Below expected level

☐ Expected level

☐ Above expected level

☐ Exceptional

Results

Your child's school will send you a report indicating his or her levels in the tests and the teacher assessment.

The school's overall test results will be included in local and national league tables, which are published in most newspapers.

What can parents do to help?

While it is never a good idea to encourage cramming, you can help your child to succeed by:

- Making sure he or she has enough food, sleep and leisure time during the test period.
- Practising important skills such as writing and reading stories, spelling and mental arithmetic.
- Telling him or her what to expect in the test, such as important symbols and key words.
- Helping him or her to be comfortable in test conditions including working within a time limit, reading questions carefully and understanding different ways of answering.

Maths at Year 4

Typical 7-year-olds attain Level 2 in Maths at the end of Year 2. By the end of Year 4, most children will be working towards Level 3. Some might be attaining a Level 3 and some very able children might attain Level 4.

Setting the tests

The written test

Allow between 45 minutes and one hour to complete the written test. If your child attempts Part B, allow longer.

Your child will need a ruler, pencil, rubber and, if possible, a small mirror or piece of tracing paper. No extra writing paper is needed. Calculators must *not* be used.

The written test is split into two parts, A and B. If your child scores highly in Part A, he or she can go on to try the harder questions in Part B. There is not a strict time limit on this test, but do not force your child to continue if he or she can no longer answer any questions.

If your child has difficulty in reading the questions, these can be read aloud, provided the mathematical words are not altered or explained. Where necessary, children can dictate their answers for you to write them down. For large numbers, however, a child should be clear which digits are intended to be written, e.g. for a number such as three thousand and six, the child must indicate that this should be written three, zero, zero, six.

The mental test

The marks scored in the national Mental Maths Test are not included when levelling at Year 4. However, in the Year 6 National Tests your child's mental scores will form part of the overall mark used for levelling.

The mental test should take approximately 10–15 minutes to give, and it is necessary for you to read aloud the questions on pages 25 and 26. Cut these pages out for this purpose. Your child will only need a pencil and rubber for the mental test.

The mental test contains a series of questions for you to read to your child and answer sheets for him or her to write answers on. Allow only the time suggested for each question and read each question twice.

Marking the tests

Next to each question is a number indicating how many marks the question or part of the question is worth. Enter your child's mark into the circle, using the answer pages to help you decide how many points to award.

Find your child's total score from the written test and refer to page 34 for information about the level your child might be working at.

Practice Pages

At the end of the book are some Practice Pages to boost your child's skills even further.

1 Look at these cards.

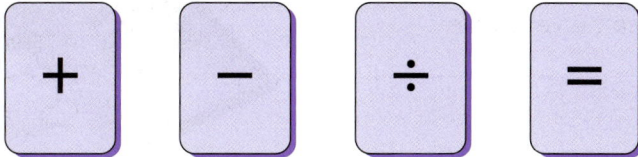

Use these cards to make correct number sentences.

You can use a card more than once.

a 24 ☐ 4 ☐ 6

1

b 25 ☐ 8 ☐ 33

1

2 Leanne is planting **31** flowers in her garden.

After planting the **eleventh** flower, how many more has she left to plant?

☐

1

TOTAL

3

3 How many

are worth the same as

£5

?

1

4 Here are some birds on a branch.

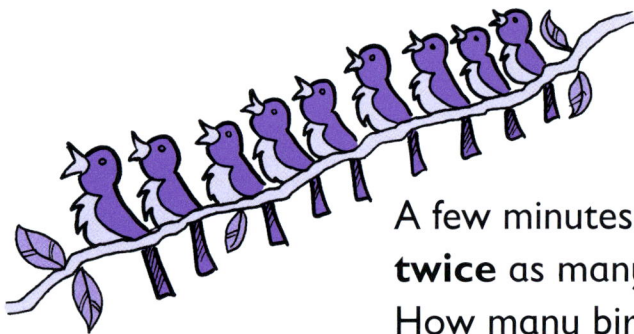

A few minutes ago there were **twice** as many birds on this branch. How many birds were on the branch?

1

5 Fill in the missing numbers.

a 76 + $\bigcirc$ = 103

1

b 92 − $\diamondsuit$ = 38

1

TOTAL

$\bigcirc$

4

6 Write the number that is half-way between these two numbers.

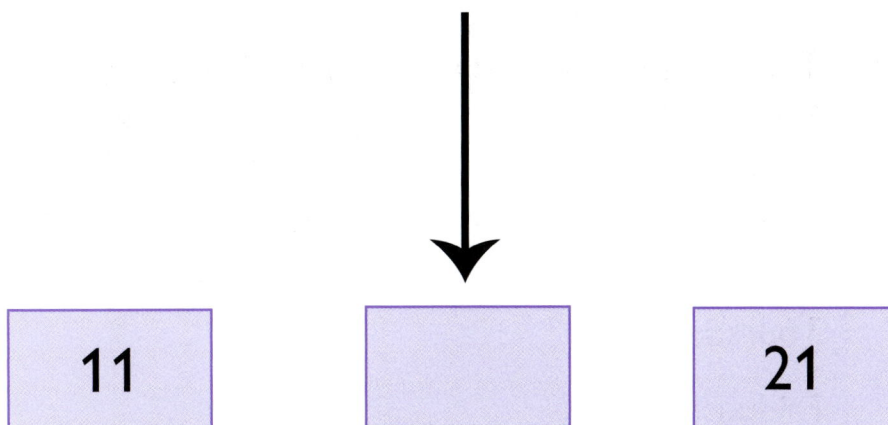

| 11 | | 21 |

7 Write these numbers in order.

| 71 | 57 | 17 | 107 | 70 |

smallest   largest

8 This table shows the number of letters Mrs Jones received each day.

Day	Number of letters
Monday	6
Tuesday	2
Wednesday	3
Thursday	8
Friday	5
Saturday	7

a On which two days did Mrs Jones get fewer than 5 letters?

1

b How many more letters did she get on Thursday than on Tuesday?

1

c What was the total number of letters Mrs Jones received during this week?

1

TOTAL

3

9 Round these numbers to the nearest ten by drawing a line to the correct circle.

73   67   84   62   75

60   70   80

1

10 Which of the shapes below is a reflection of the shaded shape? Tick your answer.

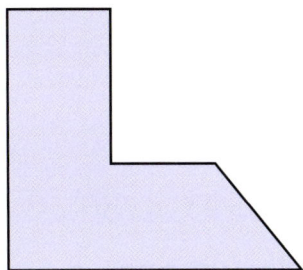

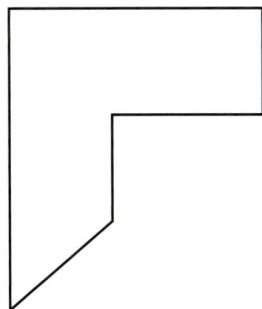

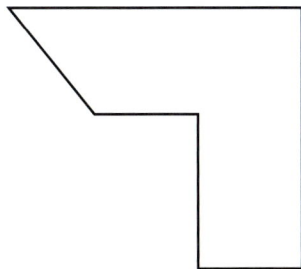

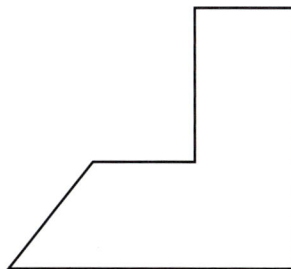

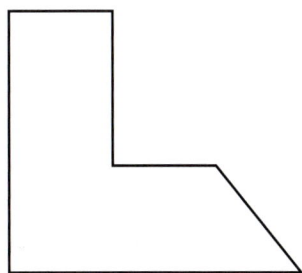

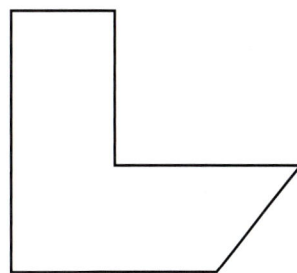

1

TOTAL

2

5

11 a Fill in the missing numbers on this **tally chart**.

Number of shells some children collected from the beach

name	tally	number of shells
Jamilla	‖‖ ‖	6
Rumi	‖‖ ‖‖ ‖‖‖	
Dean	‖‖ ‖‖ ‖‖	
Jasper	‖‖ ‖‖	
Sarah	‖‖ ‖‖	

b How many shells were collected in total?

c Part of this information has been drawn onto a graph.
Finish the graph using the tally chart above.

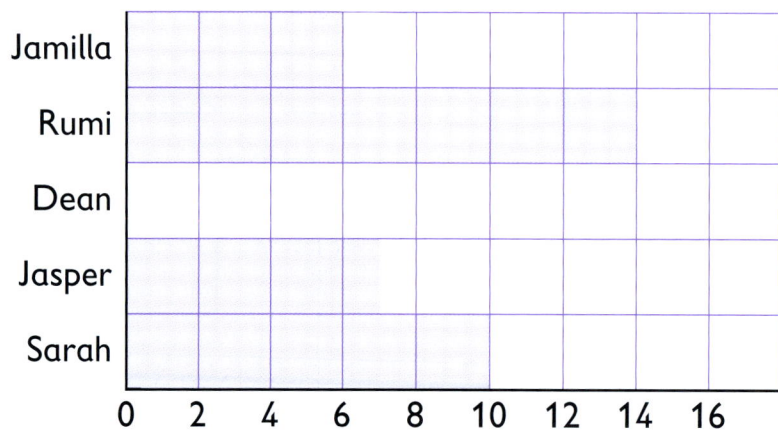

Jamilla
Rumi
Dean
Jasper
Sarah

0 2 4 6 8 10 12 14 16

1

1

1

TOTAL

3

6

28 Match the time on Big Ben to one of the digital clocks by drawing a line.

4:45

7:27

5:35

4:35

6:40

1

TOTAL

1

15

29 Join each answer to its matching question.

17	19 + 9
24	34 − 17
28	37 + 9
38	40 − 16
46	28 + 15
43	52 − 14

2

30 Shade one-tenth of this grid.

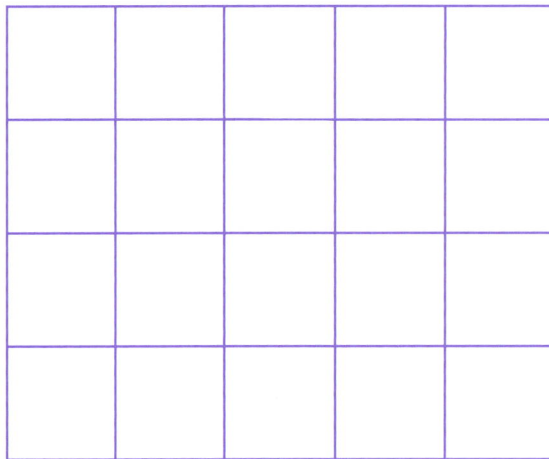

1

31 How many full $\frac{1}{2}$ **litre** cups of water will it take to fill this jug?

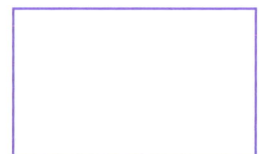

1

TOTAL

4

16

32 One of these descriptions of this shape is correct.

Tick the correct description.

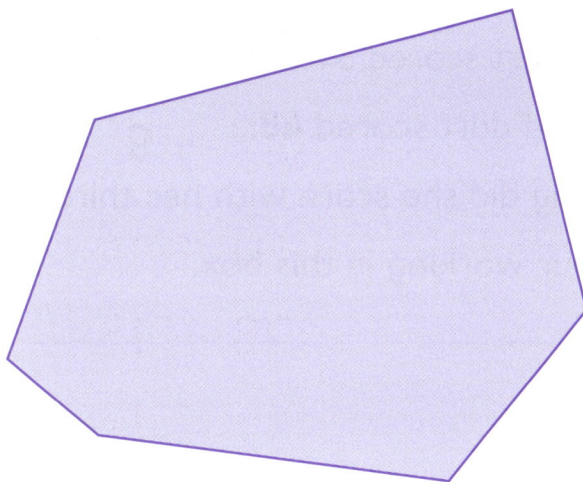

It is a pentagon with three right angles.

It is a symmetrical hexagon.

It is a hexagon with one right angle.

This shape does not have any right angles.

This shape is a hexagon with no right angles.

STOP HERE AND MARK PART A

33 Emma scored **141** with 3 darts.

Her first dart scored **57**.

Her second dart scored **48**.

How many did she score with her third dart?

Show your working in this box.

1

34 Complete this two-digit number to make a **multiple of 7**.

5	

1

35 Write the number that is exactly **half-way** between

2.6 and 3.2

1

TOTAL

3

36 One side of a square has been drawn on the grid.

a Draw the other sides to finish the square.

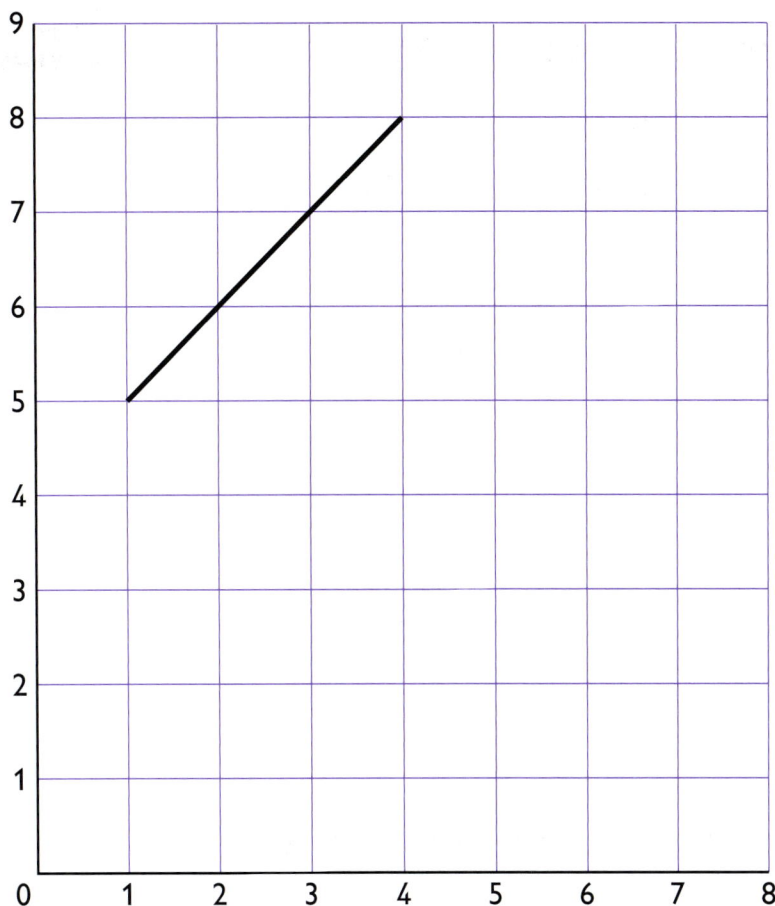

b Write the co-ordinates of the corners of the square.

(,   )   (,   )   (,   )   (,   )

1

2

TOTAL

3

37 **4.7** is marked on this number line.

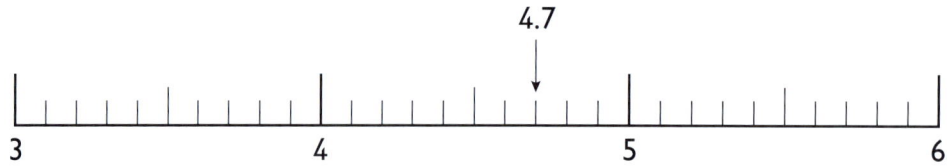

4.7

```
|_|_|_|_|_|_|_|_|_|_|_|_|_|_|_|_|_|_|_|_|_|_|_|_|_|_|_|
3           4         ↓ 5           6
```

a Mark **3.4** on the line.

1

b Mark **5.85** on the line.

1

38 Write the correct number in the IN box.

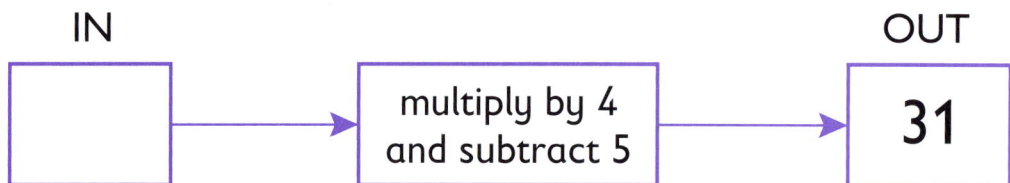

IN

OUT

multiply by 4
and subtract 5

31

1

39 Draw a ring around the amount this apple is most likely to weigh.

150 kg

10 kg

10 g

150 g

1500 g

150 kg

1

40 The street lights were lit on Wednesday at 21:36.

They were on for 11 hours and 27 minutes.

When did the lights go off?

1

41 Write the correct number in the circle.

(37) − (29) = (24) ÷ ◯

1

TOTAL

2

22

42 Write each of these letters in the correct region of this diagram.

X   S   M   E

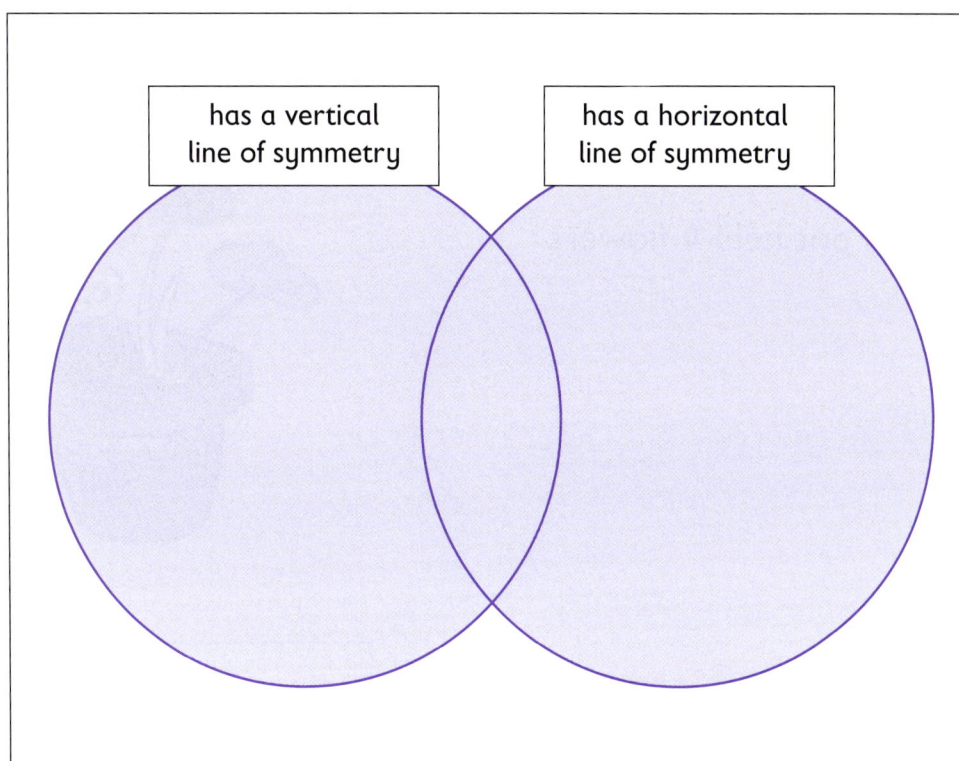

| has a vertical line of symmetry | has a horizontal line of symmetry |

2

43 The **area** of a rectangle is **36 cm²**.

The **length** of one side is **9 cm**.

What is the **perimeter** of the rectangle?

1

44 Sanjay planted **62** flowers in pots.

Each pot held **4** flowers.

a How many pots did he need?

1

b How many pots were full?

1

TOTAL

3

24

Mental Maths Test

"For this first set of questions you have five seconds to work out each answer and write it down."

1   What is double nine?

2   Three, six, nine… What comes next?

3   How many eight-pence chews can you buy with twenty-four pence?

4   Divide thirty-five pence by five.

5   Write an odd number between forty-two and fifty.

6   Add one to nine hundred and ninety-nine.

7   Sixty children get into teams of five. How many teams are there?

8   Multiply three by nine.

9   Write the number seven hundred and twelve in figures.

10   What is nought point six plus nought point five?

11   What is ten more than ninety-six?

12   Pete had a five pound note. He spent three pounds and eighty pence. How much has he now?

"For the next set of questions you have ten seconds to work out each answer and write it down."

13   Write two numbers that have a difference of sixteen.

14   Look at the answer sheet. How many small cubes have been joined to make this cuboid?

15   Look at the answer sheet. What is the perimeter of this pentagon?

16   What number is three-quarters of twenty-four?

17   How many centimetres are there in two and a half metres?

18   If two hundred sweets are shared equally between four people, how many sweets does each person get?

19   Look at the answer sheet. Circle the decimal that is equivalent to nine-tenths.

20   I'm thinking of a number. I divide it by three. My answer is twenty. What is my number?

5-second questions

1.

2.

3.

4.

5.

6.

7.

8.

9.

10.   0.6   0.5

11.

12.

1

1

1

1

1

1

1

1

1

1

1

1

TOTAL

12

10-second questions

13

14

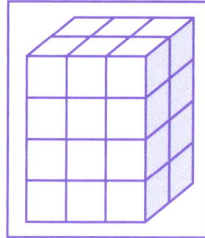

15

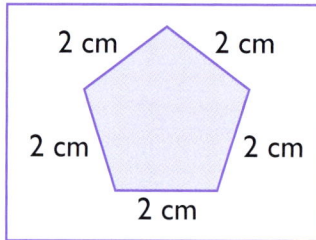

2 cm   2 cm

2 cm   2 cm

2 cm

16

17

18

19

9.0	0.9
9.10	0.910
	10.9

20

TOTAL

8

Question number	Answer	Mark	Parent's notes and additional comments
1a	$24 \div 4 = 6$ or $24 = 4 \times 6$	1	
1b	$25 + 8 = 33$	1	
2	20	1	
3	10	1	
4	18	1	
5a	$76 + \mathbf{27} = 103$	1	Some children may make the mistake of adding 76 and 103. Children need to realise that, despite having an addition sign, this question can be answered by subtracting 76 from 103.
5b	$92 - \mathbf{54} = 38$	1	
6	16	1	A useful way of finding the number half-way between two others is to add the two numbers, e.g. 11 and 21, and then halve the answer, e.g. $32 \div 2 = 16$.
7	17, 57, 70, 71, 107	1	Ask your child to read each number aloud to ensure he or she can read the numerals correctly.
8a	Tuesday, Wednesday	1	
8b	6	1	
8c	31	1	
9	$73 \rightarrow 70$ $67 \rightarrow 70$ $84 \rightarrow 80$ $62 \rightarrow 60$ $75 \rightarrow 80$	1	Remind your child that numbers ending in 5 are rounded up.
10	The third shape: 	1	Children can use a mirror or tracing paper to help them with this question.
11a	Column of tally chart filled in as follows: 6 **14** **15** 7 **10** All answers must be correct.	1	
11b	52	1	
11c	Dean's row should show 15 shells ($7\frac{1}{2}$ squares).	1	

Answers

Question number	Answer	Mark	Parent's notes and additional comments
12		1	Children can use a mirror or tracing paper to help them with this question.
13	405	1	Any non-calculator method can be used to find the answer.
14	25	1	Any non-calculator method can be used to find the answer.
15	325 g	1	Mass is the correct word to use when finding how heavy something is. Children may have been using the word 'weight' instead of 'mass' in earlier years.
16	9	1	
17	A line drawn that is 7 cm long. Allow up to 2 mm for error.	1	
18	A ring around 3 drawing pins.	1	
19a	9765	1	Use number cards to practise this type of question. Give your child several cards and ask him or her to make two-, three- or four-digit numbers greater (more) than or less than a given number, or lying between two e.g. between 4000 and 6000. Ask him or her to make odd or even numbers or those divisible by 2, 5 or 10.
19b	5679	1	
19c	6795, 6975, 7695, 7965, 9765 or 9675	1	
19d	5796, 5769, 5976, 5967, 5679, 5697, 6975, 6957, 6795, 6759, 6579 or 6597	1	
20	804	1	Any non-calculator method can be used to find the answer.
21	483 → 500 648 → 600 591 → 600 353 → 400	1	Remind your child that numbers with 5 in the tens column are rounded up.
22	£6.18	1	Note that amounts of money should never be written with both the £ sign and a p sign, e.g. £6.18p is incorrect and would not earn a mark.

Question number	Answer	Mark	Parent's notes and additional comments
23	288, 144, **72, 36, 18**	1	
24	$200 - (5 \times 32)$	1	
25	3700	1	
26	Any numbers of 50p and 20p coins totalling £7.60, e.g. 14 × 50p and 3 × 20p.	1	
27	Pentagon (a five-sided shape) with at least 2 right angles, e.g.:	1	
28	5:35	1	Discuss the different ways of showing or describing the times on a clock, e.g. 7:40 can be described as 'seven forty', 'twenty to eight' or 'twenty minutes to eight' and can be shown on a traditional clock face or in digital form.
29	$17 = 34 - 17$ $24 = 40 - 16$ $28 = 19 + 9$ $38 = 52 - 14$ $46 = 37 + 9$ $43 = 28 + 15$ Award one mark if all but two matches are correct.	2	
30	Any 2 squares of the grid shaded. (Award a mark if part squares are shaded provided the total is 2 squares.)	1	One-tenth of 20 squares is 2 squares. Encourage your child to find one-tenth by dividing by 10.
31	12	1	
32	It is a hexagon with one right angle.	1	

Answers

Question number	Answer	Mark	Parent's notes and additional comments
33	36	1	Any non-calculator method can be used to find the answer.
34	56	1	A multiple is a number that can be exactly divided by another with no remainder.
35	2.9	1	A useful way of finding the number half-way between two others is to add the two numbers, e.g. 2.6 and 3.2, and then halve the answer, e.g. $5.8 \div 2 = 2.9$.
36a	The new corners (vertices) must be positioned at (4, 2) and (7, 5).	1	
36b	(1, 5) (4, 8) (7, 5) (4, 2) These co-ordinates can be written in any order. Award one mark if only one is incorrect.	2	Remind your child that the first co-ordinate tells you how many across and the second tells you how many up (or down). Use the phrase 'Into the house and up the stairs' to help your child remember the order.
37a		1	
37b		1	
38	9	1	
39	150 g	1	
40	09:03 *or* 9:03	1	Here children are required to be familiar with the twenty-four hour clock.
41	$37 - 29 = 24 \div 3$	1	Children sometimes make mistakes with this type of question as they do not fully understand the meaning of the equals sign ($=$). Some children incorrectly view it as an 'answer giver' and will say that $37 - 29$ does not give the answer 24. Show your child that the equals sign stands for 'is the same value as', to demonstrate that the answer to one side of the number sentence is the same as the answer to the other side.
42	Award one mark if three out of four letters are correctly positioned.	2	
43	26 cm	1	The area of a rectangle can be found by multiplying its length by its width. If the area is 36 cm² and the length of one side is 9 cm, the other side (its width) must be 4 cm as 9 cm $\times$ 4 cm = 36 cm². The perimeter is the distance all the way around the edge of the shape. To find the perimeter of this rectangle, add up the lengths of the four sides, 9 cm + 9 cm + 4 cm + 4 cm = 26 cm.
44a	16	1	
44b	15	1	

1 18

2 12

3 3

4 7

5 43, 45, 47 *or* 49

6 1000 *or* one thousand

7 12

8 27

9 712

10 1.1

11 106

12 £1.20 *or* 120p

13 Any two numbers with a difference of 16, e.g. 1 and 17, 15 and 31, etc.

14 24

15 10 cm

16 18

17 250 cm

18 50

19 0.9

20 60

Award one mark per correct answer.

National Curriculum Levels

The test in Year 4 has a Part A and a Part B.

The score is out of a maximum of 59 marks (42 marks for Part A and 17 for Part B).

If your child has scored highly in Part A, he or she can go on to try the harder questions in Part B.

Write your child's scores below:

Mark scored in Part A ☐ out of 42

Mark scored in Part B ☐ out of 17

Total ☐ out of 59

Children at Year 4 complete a test of this type and from this each child can be levelled and graded according to his or her total score. The children do not sit a formal Mental Maths Test at this stage.

Total marks 59

Mark	0–10	11–15	16–20	21–26	27–31	32–36	37–41	42–59
Level	Below Level 2	Level 2C	Level 2B	Level 2A	Level 3C	Level 3B	Level 3A	Level 4

If a child scores very highly on the test, there is a possibility of sitting the Year 5 or 6 tests, to gain clearer information about the extent to which he or she is performing at Level 4.

NUMBER AND ALGEBRA

1 Find the answers:

$57 + 14 =$ $28 + 79 =$

$189 + 245 =$ $134 + 749 =$

$91 - 38 =$ $82 - 43 =$

$778 - 364 =$ $626 - 389 =$

$8 \times 3 =$ $6 \times 4 =$

$13 \times 3 =$ $15 \times 5 =$

$27 \div 3 =$ $35 \div 5 =$

$36 \div 4 =$ $36 \div 3 =$

2 Fill in the missing signs. $+$ $-$ $\times$ $\div$

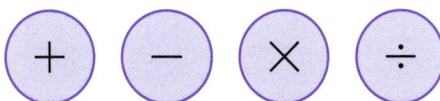

$16 \bigcirc 4 = 4$ $34 \bigcirc 28 = 6$

$125 \bigcirc 25 = 150$ $14 \bigcirc 3 = 42$

$100 \bigcirc 25 = 4$ $103 \bigcirc 5 = 98$

$24 \bigcirc 1 \bigcirc 5 = 5$

$33 \bigcirc 3 \bigcirc 5 = 6$

NUMBER AND ALGEBRA

3   Fill in the missing numbers.

$27 \div \boxed{} = 3$

$4 \times \boxed{} = 44$

$37 - 11 = 15 + \boxed{}$

$6 + 27 = 40 - \boxed{}$

4   Continue these patterns:

3, 6, 9, 12, $\boxed{}$ $\boxed{}$ $\boxed{}$

95, 96, 97, 98, $\boxed{}$ $\boxed{}$ $\boxed{}$

0, 25, 50, 75, $\boxed{}$ $\boxed{}$ $\boxed{}$

212, 211, 210, $\boxed{}$ $\boxed{}$ $\boxed{}$

4002, 4001, 4000, $\boxed{}$ $\boxed{}$ $\boxed{}$

NUMBER AND ALGEBRA

5 **Halve**:

18	26	70
120	68	150
52	78	144

Double:

8	12	25
40	150	34
72	59	135

6 Answer these word questions.

A magazine costs £1.20.
How much does it cost for two magazines?

£ _____

A camera film costs £3.68.
How much does it cost for two films?

£ _____

24 eggs are put into boxes of six.
How many boxes will be filled?

_____ boxes

How many 20 cm lengths of ribbon
can be cut from a length of 100 cm?

_____ lengths

I have 66 pence. How many 6p chews
can I buy?

_____ chews

SHAPE, SPACE AND MEASURES

7   Shade four more squares to make this pattern symmetrical.

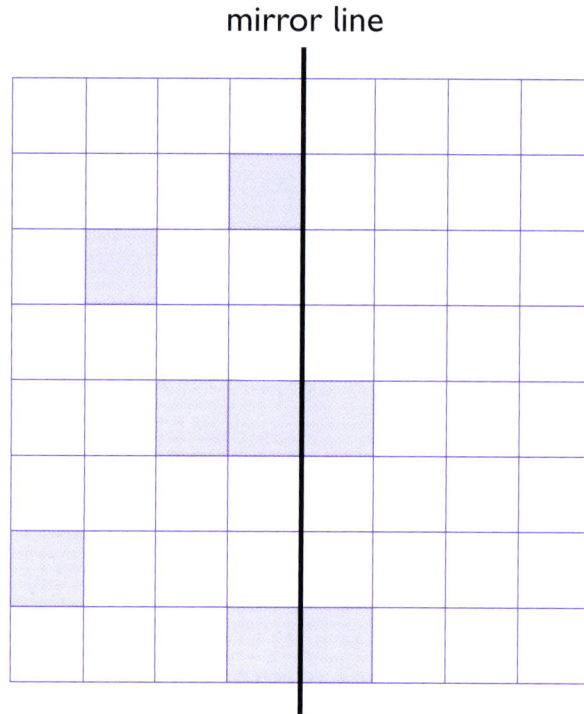

mirror line

8   Draw and label a **hexagon**, a **pentagon** and an **octagon** on this grid.

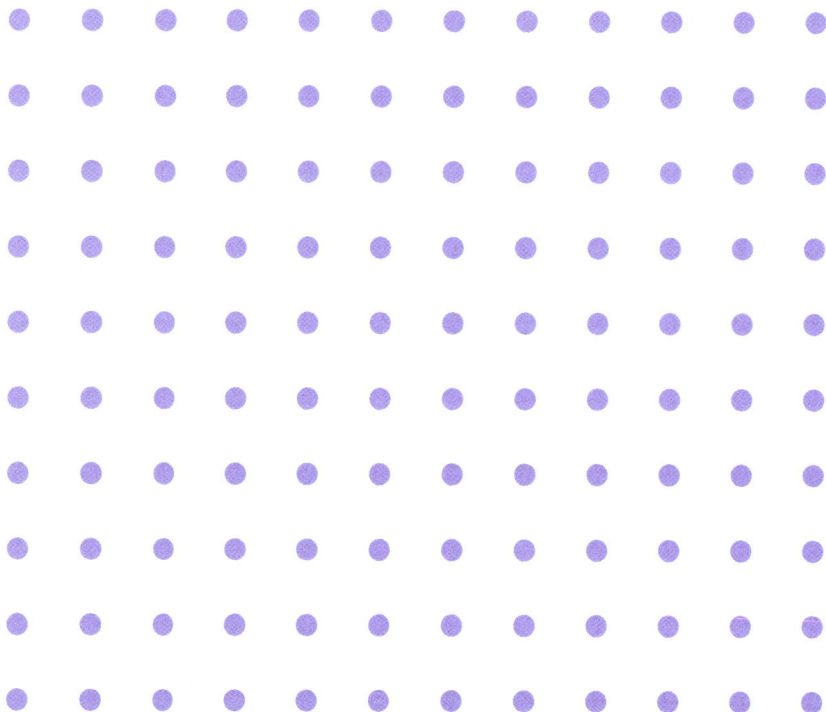

SHAPE, SPACE AND MEASURES

9 Write the times shown on these clocks in digital form.

10 Draw the hands of the clocks to show these times.

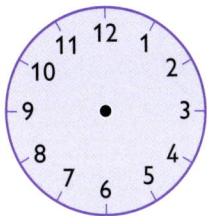

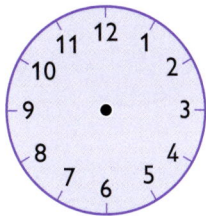

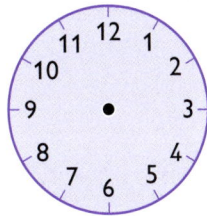

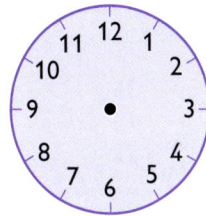

| 1:30 | 8:15 | 11:35 | 6:50 |

11 Which numbers are the arrows pointing to?

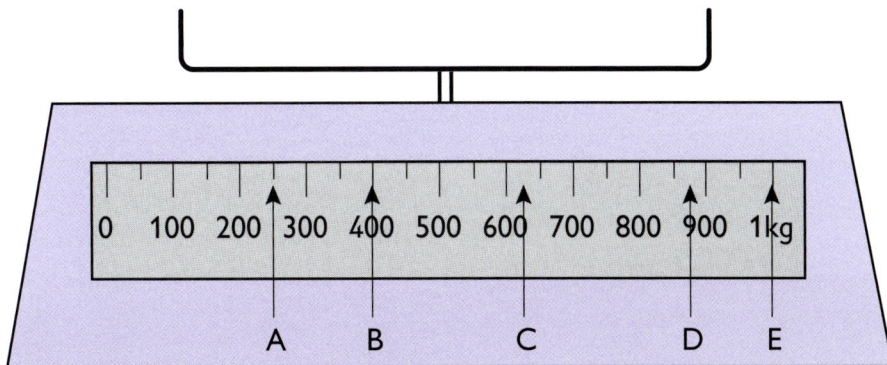

0   100   200   300   400   500   600   700   800   900   1kg

A   B   C   D   E

A ☐   B ☐   C ☐   D ☐   E ☐

Answers

1
71	107
434	883
53	39
414	237
24	24
39	75
9	7
9	12

2
÷   −
+   ×
÷   −
+, ÷
−, ÷ or ÷, −

3
9
11
11
7

4
15, 18, 21
99, 100, 101
100, 125, 150
209, 208, 207
3999, 3998, 3997

5
9	13	35
60	34	75
26	39	72
16	24	50
80	300	68
144	118	270

6
£2.40
£7.36
4
5
11

7
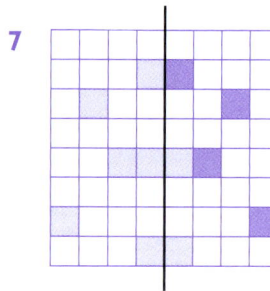

8 Labelled hexagon (6 straight sides)
Labelled pentagon (5 straight sides)
Labelled octagon (8 straight sides)

9 12:15   4:30   7:20   10:55
(or in 24-hour clock time)

10
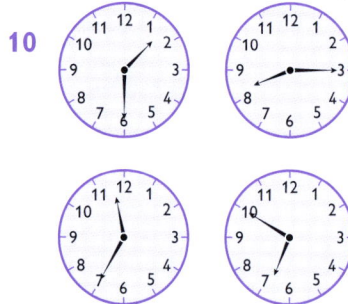

11 250 g, 400 g, 625 g, 875 g,
1 kg (or 1000 g)

Notes